LAZY IN NATURE

HIKING JOURNAL

THE BEST MEMORIES

THE JOURNEY OF A THOUSAND MILES
BEGINS WITH A SINGLE STEP

- LAO TZO

LAZY IN NATURE™
Hiking Journal

Published by Lighthouse Manuscripts LLC
12020 Sunrise Valley Drive, Suite 100
Reston, VA 20191

ISBN: 978-1-7358723-9-1

Printed in the United States of America

For more information, email: info@lighthousemanuscripts.com or support@lazyinnature.com

HIKING JOURNAL

THE BEST MEMORIES

LAZY IN NATURE

DATE:

LOCATION:

TRAIL INFORMATION

- Trail Name:
- Trail Type:
- Trail Distance:
- Altitude:
- Terrain Level:
- Entry/Parking Fees:
- Water Availability:
- Cell Phone Signal:

DETAILS

Weather/Temp:

Start Day/Time:

End Day/Time:

First Visit:

Return Visit:

Hiking Difficulty:

Hiking Rate:

☆ ☆ ☆ ☆ ☆

HIKING PARTNER(S)	CONTACT INFO

ADDITIONAL TRAIL NOTES

DATE: | LOCATION:

TRAIL INFORMATION

- Trail Name:
- Trail Type:
- Trail Distance:
- Altitude:
- Terrain Level:
- Entry/Parking Fees:
- Water Availability:
- Cell Phone Signal:

DETAILS

Weather/Temp:

Start Day/Time:

End Day/Time:

First Visit:

Return Visit:

Hiking Difficulty:

Hiking Rate:

☆ ☆ ☆ ☆ ☆

HIKING PARTNER(S)

CONTACT INFO

ADDITIONAL TRAIL NOTES

DATE:

LOCATION:

TRAIL INFORMATION

- Trail Name:
- Trail Type:
- Trail Distance:
- Altitude:
- Terrain Level:
- Entry/Parking Fees:
- Water Availability:
- Cell Phone Signal:

DETAILS

Weather/Temp:

Start Day/Time:

End Day/Time:

First Visit:

Return Visit:

Hiking Difficulty:

Hiking Rate:

☆ ☆ ☆ ☆ ☆

HIKING PARTNER(S)

CONTACT INFO

ADDITIONAL TRAIL NOTES

DATE:

LOCATION:

TRAIL INFORMATION

- Trail Name:
- Trail Type:
- Trail Distance:
- Altitude:
- Terrain Level:
- Entry/Parking Fees:
- Water Availability:
- Cell Phone Signal:

DETAILS

Weather/Temp:

Start Day/Time:

End Day/Time:

First Visit:

Return Visit:

Hiking Difficulty:

Hiking Rate:

☆ ☆ ☆ ☆ ☆

HIKING PARTNER(S)	CONTACT INFO

ADDITIONAL TRAIL NOTES

DATE:

LOCATION:

TRAIL INFORMATION

- Trail Name:
- Trail Type:
- Trail Distance:
- Altitude:
- Terrain Level:
- Entry/Parking Fees:
- Water Availability:
- Cell Phone Signal:

DETAILS

Weather/Temp:

Start Day/Time:

End Day/Time:

First Visit:

Return Visit:

Hiking Difficulty:

Hiking Rate:

☆ ☆ ☆ ☆ ☆

HIKING PARTNER(S)

CONTACT INFO

ADDITIONAL TRAIL NOTES

DATE: *LOCATION:*

TRAIL INFORMATION

- Trail Name:
- Trail Type:
- Trail Distance:
- Altitude:
- Terrain Level:
- Entry/Parking Fees:
- Water Availability:
- Cell Phone Signal:

DETAILS

Weather/Temp:

Start Day/Time:

End Day/Time:

First Visit:

Return Visit:

Hiking Difficulty:

Hiking Rate:

☆ ☆ ☆ ☆ ☆

HIKING PARTNER(S)	*CONTACT INFO*

ADDITIONAL TRAIL NOTES

DATE:

LOCATION:

TRAIL INFORMATION

- Trail Name:
- Trail Type:
- Trail Distance:
- Altitude:
- Terrain Level:
- Entry/Parking Fees:
- Water Availability:
- Cell Phone Signal:

DETAILS

Weather/Temp:

Start Day/Time:

End Day/Time:

First Visit:

Return Visit:

Hiking Difficulty:

Hiking Rate:

☆ ☆ ☆ ☆ ☆

HIKING PARTNER(S)	CONTACT INFO

ADDITIONAL TRAIL NOTES

DATE:

LOCATION:

TRAIL INFORMATION

- Trail Name:
- Trail Type:
- Trail Distance:
- Altitude:
- Terrain Level:
- Entry/Parking Fees:
- Water Availability:
- Cell Phone Signal:

DETAILS

Weather/Temp:

Start Day/Time:

End Day/Time:

First Visit:

Return Visit:

Hiking Difficulty:

Hiking Rate:

☆ ☆ ☆ ☆ ☆

HIKING PARTNER(S)	CONTACT INFO

ADDITIONAL TRAIL NOTES

DATE:

LOCATION:

TRAIL INFORMATION

- Trail Name:
- Trail Type:
- Trail Distance:
- Altitude:
- Terrain Level:
- Entry/Parking Fees:
- Water Availability:
- Cell Phone Signal:

DETAILS

Weather/Temp:

Start Day/Time:

End Day/Time:

First Visit:

Return Visit:

Hiking Difficulty:

Hiking Rate:

☆　☆　☆　☆　☆

HIKING PARTNER(S)

CONTACT INFO

ADDITIONAL TRAIL NOTES

DATE:

LOCATION:

TRAIL INFORMATION

- Trail Name:
- Trail Type:
- Trail Distance:
- Altitude:
- Terrain Level:
- Entry/Parking Fees:
- Water Availability:
- Cell Phone Signal:

DETAILS

Weather/Temp:

Start Day/Time:

End Day/Time:

First Visit:

Return Visit:

Hiking Difficulty:

Hiking Rate:

☆ ☆ ☆ ☆ ☆

HIKING PARTNER(S)

CONTACT INFO

ADDITIONAL TRAIL NOTES

DATE:

LOCATION:

TRAIL INFORMATION

- Trail Name:
- Trail Type:
- Trail Distance:
- Altitude:
- Terrain Level:
- Entry/Parking Fees:
- Water Availability:
- Cell Phone Signal:

DETAILS

Weather/Temp:

Start Day/Time:

End Day/Time:

First Visit:

Return Visit:

Hiking Difficulty:

Hiking Rate:

☆ ☆ ☆ ☆ ☆

HIKING PARTNER(S)

CONTACT INFO

ADDITIONAL TRAIL NOTES

DATE:

LOCATION:

TRAIL INFORMATION

🔥 Trail Name:

🔥 Trail Type:

🔥 Trail Distance:

🔥 Altitude:

🔥 Terrain Level:

🔥 Entry/Parking Fees:

🔥 Water Availability:

🔥 Cell Phone Signal:

DETAILS

Weather/Temp:

Start Day/Time:

End Day/Time:

First Visit:

Return Visit:

Hiking Difficulty:

Hiking Rate:

☆ ☆ ☆ ☆ ☆

HIKING PARTNER(S)

CONTACT INFO

ADDITIONAL TRAIL NOTES

DATE:

LOCATION:

TRAIL INFORMATION

- Trail Name:
- Trail Type:
- Trail Distance:
- Altitude:
- Terrain Level:
- Entry/Parking Fees:
- Water Availability:
- Cell Phone Signal:

DETAILS

Weather/Temp:

Start Day/Time:

End Day/Time:

First Visit:

Return Visit:

Hiking Difficulty:

Hiking Rate:

☆　　☆　　☆　　☆　　☆

HIKING PARTNER(S)	CONTACT INFO

ADDITIONAL TRAIL NOTES

DATE:

LOCATION:

TRAIL INFORMATION

- Trail Name:
- Trail Type:
- Trail Distance:
- Altitude:
- Terrain Level:
- Entry/Parking Fees:
- Water Availability:
- Cell Phone Signal:

DETAILS

Weather/Temp:

Start Day/Time:

End Day/Time:

First Visit:

Return Visit:

Hiking Difficulty:

Hiking Rate:

☆ ☆ ☆ ☆ ☆

HIKING PARTNER(S)

CONTACT INFO

ADDITIONAL TRAIL NOTES

DATE:

LOCATION:

TRAIL INFORMATION

- Trail Name:
- Trail Type:
- Trail Distance:
- Altitude:
- Terrain Level:
- Entry/Parking Fees:
- Water Availability:
- Cell Phone Signal:

DETAILS

Weather/Temp:

Start Day/Time:

End Day/Time:

First Visit:

Return Visit:

Hiking Difficulty:

Hiking Rate:

☆ ☆ ☆ ☆ ☆

HIKING PARTNER(S)

CONTACT INFO

ADDITIONAL TRAIL NOTES

DATE:

LOCATION:

TRAIL INFORMATION

- Trail Name:
- Trail Type:
- Trail Distance:
- Altitude:
- Terrain Level:
- Entry/Parking Fees:
- Water Availability:
- Cell Phone Signal:

DETAILS

Weather/Temp:

Start Day/Time:

End Day/Time:

First Visit:

Return Visit:

Hiking Difficulty:

Hiking Rate:

☆ ☆ ☆ ☆ ☆

HIKING PARTNER(S)

CONTACT INFO

ADDITIONAL TRAIL NOTES

DATE:

LOCATION:

TRAIL INFORMATION

- Trail Name:
- Trail Type:
- Trail Distance:
- Altitude:
- Terrain Level:
- Entry/Parking Fees:
- Water Availability:
- Cell Phone Signal:

DETAILS

Weather/Temp:

Start Day/Time:

End Day/Time:

First Visit:

Return Visit:

Hiking Difficulty:

Hiking Rate:

☆ ☆ ☆ ☆ ☆

HIKING PARTNER(S)

CONTACT INFO

ADDITIONAL TRAIL NOTES

DATE:

LOCATION:

TRAIL INFORMATION

- Trail Name:
- Trail Type:
- Trail Distance:
- Altitude:
- Terrain Level:
- Entry/Parking Fees:
- Water Availability:
- Cell Phone Signal:

DETAILS

Weather/Temp:

Start Day/Time:

End Day/Time:

First Visit:

Return Visit:

Hiking Difficulty:

Hiking Rate:

☆ ☆ ☆ ☆ ☆

HIKING PARTNER(S)

CONTACT INFO

ADDITIONAL TRAIL NOTES

DATE:

LOCATION:

TRAIL INFORMATION

- Trail Name:
- Trail Type:
- Trail Distance:
- Altitude:
- Terrain Level:
- Entry/Parking Fees:
- Water Availability:
- Cell Phone Signal:

DETAILS

Weather/Temp:

Start Day/Time:

End Day/Time:

First Visit:

Return Visit:

Hiking Difficulty:

Hiking Rate:

☆　☆　☆　☆　☆

HIKING PARTNER(S)	CONTACT INFO

ADDITIONAL TRAIL NOTES

DATE:

LOCATION:

TRAIL INFORMATION

- Trail Name:
- Trail Type:
- Trail Distance:
- Altitude:
- Terrain Level:
- Entry/Parking Fees:
- Water Availability:
- Cell Phone Signal:

DETAILS

Weather/Temp:

Start Day/Time:

End Day/Time:

First Visit:

Return Visit:

Hiking Difficulty:

Hiking Rate:

☆ ☆ ☆ ☆ ☆

HIKING PARTNER(S)

CONTACT INFO

ADDITIONAL TRAIL NOTES

DATE:

LOCATION:

TRAIL INFORMATION

- Trail Name:
- Trail Type:
- Trail Distance:
- Altitude:
- Terrain Level:
- Entry/Parking Fees:
- Water Availability:
- Cell Phone Signal:

DETAILS

Weather/Temp:

Start Day/Time:

End Day/Time:

First Visit:

Return Visit:

Hiking Difficulty:

Hiking Rate:

☆ ☆ ☆ ☆ ☆

HIKING PARTNER(S)

CONTACT INFO

ADDITIONAL TRAIL NOTES

DATE:

LOCATION:

TRAIL INFORMATION

- Trail Name:
- Trail Type:
- Trail Distance:
- Altitude:
- Terrain Level:
- Entry/Parking Fees:
- Water Availability:
- Cell Phone Signal:

DETAILS

Weather/Temp:

Start Day/Time:

End Day/Time:

First Visit:

Return Visit:

Hiking Difficulty:

Hiking Rate:

☆ ☆ ☆ ☆ ☆

HIKING PARTNER(S)

CONTACT INFO

ADDITIONAL TRAIL NOTES

DATE:

LOCATION:

TRAIL INFORMATION

- Trail Name:
- Trail Type:
- Trail Distance:
- Altitude:
- Terrain Level:
- Entry/Parking Fees:
- Water Availability:
- Cell Phone Signal:

DETAILS

Weather/Temp:

Start Day/Time:

End Day/Time:

First Visit:

Return Visit:

Hiking Difficulty:

Hiking Rate:

☆ ☆ ☆ ☆ ☆

HIKING PARTNER(S)	CONTACT INFO

ADDITIONAL TRAIL NOTES

DATE:

LOCATION:

TRAIL INFORMATION

- Trail Name:
- Trail Type:
- Trail Distance:
- Altitude:
- Terrain Level:
- Entry/Parking Fees:
- Water Availability:
- Cell Phone Signal:

DETAILS

Weather/Temp:

Start Day/Time:

End Day/Time:

First Visit:

Return Visit:

Hiking Difficulty:

Hiking Rate:

☆ ☆ ☆ ☆ ☆

HIKING PARTNER(S)

CONTACT INFO

ADDITIONAL TRAIL NOTES

DATE:

LOCATION:

TRAIL INFORMATION

- Trail Name:
- Trail Type:
- Trail Distance:
- Altitude:
- Terrain Level:
- Entry/Parking Fees:
- Water Availability:
- Cell Phone Signal:

DETAILS

Weather/Temp:

Start Day/Time:

End Day/Time:

First Visit:

Return Visit:

Hiking Difficulty:

Hiking Rate:

☆ ☆ ☆ ☆ ☆

HIKING PARTNER(S)

CONTACT INFO

ADDITIONAL TRAIL NOTES

DATE:

LOCATION:

TRAIL INFORMATION

- Trail Name:
- Trail Type:
- Trail Distance:
- Altitude:
- Terrain Level:
- Entry/Parking Fees:
- Water Availability:
- Cell Phone Signal:

DETAILS

Weather/Temp:

Start Day/Time:

End Day/Time:

First Visit:

Return Visit:

Hiking Difficulty:

Hiking Rate:

☆ ☆ ☆ ☆ ☆

HIKING PARTNER(S)	CONTACT INFO

ADDITIONAL TRAIL NOTES

DATE:

LOCATION:

TRAIL INFORMATION

- Trail Name:
- Trail Type:
- Trail Distance:
- Altitude:
- Terrain Level:
- Entry/Parking Fees:
- Water Availability:
- Cell Phone Signal:

DETAILS

Weather/Temp:

Start Day/Time:

End Day/Time:

First Visit:

Return Visit:

Hiking Difficulty:

Hiking Rate:

☆ ☆ ☆ ☆ ☆

HIKING PARTNER(S)

CONTACT INFO

ADDITIONAL TRAIL NOTES

DATE:

LOCATION:

TRAIL INFORMATION

- Trail Name:
- Trail Type:
- Trail Distance:
- Altitude:
- Terrain Level:
- Entry/Parking Fees:
- Water Availability:
- Cell Phone Signal:

DETAILS

Weather/Temp:

Start Day/Time:

End Day/Time:

First Visit:

Return Visit:

Hiking Difficulty:

Hiking Rate:

☆　　☆　　☆　　☆　　☆

HIKING PARTNER(S)	CONTACT INFO

ADDITIONAL TRAIL NOTES

DATE:

LOCATION:

TRAIL INFORMATION

- Trail Name:
- Trail Type:
- Trail Distance:
- Altitude:
- Terrain Level:
- Entry/Parking Fees:
- Water Availability:
- Cell Phone Signal:

DETAILS

Weather/Temp:

Start Day/Time:

End Day/Time:

First Visit:

Return Visit:

Hiking Difficulty:

Hiking Rate:

☆ ☆ ☆ ☆ ☆

HIKING PARTNER(S)

CONTACT INFO

ADDITIONAL TRAIL NOTES

DATE:

LOCATION:

TRAIL INFORMATION

- Trail Name:
- Trail Type:
- Trail Distance:
- Altitude:
- Terrain Level:
- Entry/Parking Fees:
- Water Availability:
- Cell Phone Signal:

DETAILS

Weather/Temp:

Start Day/Time:

End Day/Time:

First Visit:

Return Visit:

Hiking Difficulty:

Hiking Rate:

☆ ☆ ☆ ☆ ☆

HIKING PARTNER(S)

CONTACT INFO

ADDITIONAL TRAIL NOTES

DATE:

LOCATION:

TRAIL INFORMATION

- Trail Name:
- Trail Type:
- Trail Distance:
- Altitude:
- Terrain Level:
- Entry/Parking Fees:
- Water Availability:
- Cell Phone Signal:

DETAILS

Weather/Temp:

Start Day/Time:

End Day/Time:

First Visit:

Return Visit:

Hiking Difficulty:

Hiking Rate:

☆ ☆ ☆ ☆ ☆

HIKING PARTNER(S)

CONTACT INFO

ADDITIONAL TRAIL NOTES

DATE:

LOCATION:

TRAIL INFORMATION

- Trail Name:
- Trail Type:
- Trail Distance:
- Altitude:
- Terrain Level:
- Entry/Parking Fees:
- Water Availability:
- Cell Phone Signal:

DETAILS

Weather/Temp:

Start Day/Time:

End Day/Time:

First Visit:

Return Visit:

Hiking Difficulty:

Hiking Rate:

☆   ☆   ☆   ☆   ☆

HIKING PARTNER(S)

CONTACT INFO

ADDITIONAL TRAIL NOTES

DATE:

LOCATION:

TRAIL INFORMATION

- Trail Name:
- Trail Type:
- Trail Distance:
- Altitude:
- Terrain Level:
- Entry/Parking Fees:
- Water Availability:
- Cell Phone Signal:

DETAILS

Weather/Temp:

Start Day/Time:

End Day/Time:

First Visit:

Return Visit:

Hiking Difficulty:

Hiking Rate:

☆　☆　☆　☆　☆

HIKING PARTNER(S)

CONTACT INFO

ADDITIONAL TRAIL NOTES

DATE:

LOCATION:

TRAIL INFORMATION

- Trail Name:
- Trail Type:
- Trail Distance:
- Altitude:
- Terrain Level:
- Entry/Parking Fees:
- Water Availability:
- Cell Phone Signal:

DETAILS

Weather/Temp:

Start Day/Time:

End Day/Time:

First Visit:

Return Visit:

Hiking Difficulty:

Hiking Rate:

☆ ☆ ☆ ☆ ☆

HIKING PARTNER(S)

CONTACT INFO

ADDITIONAL TRAIL NOTES

DATE:

LOCATION:

TRAIL INFORMATION

- Trail Name:
- Trail Type:
- Trail Distance:
- Altitude:
- Terrain Level:
- Entry/Parking Fees:
- Water Availability:
- Cell Phone Signal:

DETAILS

Weather/Temp:

Start Day/Time:

End Day/Time:

First Visit:

Return Visit:

Hiking Difficulty:

Hiking Rate:

☆ ☆ ☆ ☆ ☆

HIKING PARTNER(S)	CONTACT INFO

ADDITIONAL TRAIL NOTES

DATE:

LOCATION:

TRAIL INFORMATION

- Trail Name:
- Trail Type:
- Trail Distance:
- Altitude:
- Terrain Level:
- Entry/Parking Fees:
- Water Availability:
- Cell Phone Signal:

DETAILS

Weather/Temp:

Start Day/Time:

End Day/Time:

First Visit:

Return Visit:

Hiking Difficulty:

Hiking Rate:

☆ ☆ ☆ ☆ ☆

HIKING PARTNER(S)

CONTACT INFO

ADDITIONAL TRAIL NOTES

DATE:

LOCATION:

TRAIL INFORMATION

Trail Name:

Trail Type:

Trail Distance:

Altitude:

Terrain Level:

Entry/Parking Fees:

Water Availability:

Cell Phone Signal:

DETAILS

Weather/Temp:

Start Day/Time:

End Day/Time:

First Visit:

Return Visit:

Hiking Difficulty:

Hiking Rate:

☆ ☆ ☆ ☆ ☆

HIKING PARTNER(S)

CONTACT INFO

ADDITIONAL TRAIL NOTES

DATE:

LOCATION:

TRAIL INFORMATION

- Trail Name:
- Trail Type:
- Trail Distance:
- Altitude:
- Terrain Level:
- Entry/Parking Fees:
- Water Availability:
- Cell Phone Signal:

DETAILS

Weather/Temp:

Start Day/Time:

End Day/Time:

First Visit:

Return Visit:

Hiking Difficulty:

Hiking Rate:

☆ ☆ ☆ ☆ ☆

HIKING PARTNER(S)	*CONTACT INFO*

ADDITIONAL TRAIL NOTES

DATE:

LOCATION:

TRAIL INFORMATION

- Trail Name:
- Trail Type:
- Trail Distance:
- Altitude:
- Terrain Level:
- Entry/Parking Fees:
- Water Availability:
- Cell Phone Signal:

DETAILS

Weather/Temp:

Start Day/Time:

End Day/Time:

First Visit:

Return Visit:

Hiking Difficulty:

Hiking Rate:

☆ ☆ ☆ ☆ ☆

HIKING PARTNER(S)

CONTACT INFO

ADDITIONAL TRAIL NOTES

DATE:

LOCATION:

TRAIL INFORMATION

- Trail Name:
- Trail Type:
- Trail Distance:
- Altitude:
- Terrain Level:
- Entry/Parking Fees:
- Water Availability:
- Cell Phone Signal:

DETAILS

Weather/Temp:

Start Day/Time:

End Day/Time:

First Visit:

Return Visit:

Hiking Difficulty:

Hiking Rate:

☆ ☆ ☆ ☆ ☆

HIKING PARTNER(S)

CONTACT INFO

ADDITIONAL TRAIL NOTES

DATE:

LOCATION:

TRAIL INFORMATION

- Trail Name:
- Trail Type:
- Trail Distance:
- Altitude:
- Terrain Level:
- Entry/Parking Fees:
- Water Availability:
- Cell Phone Signal:

DETAILS

Weather/Temp:

Start Day/Time:

End Day/Time:

First Visit:

Return Visit:

Hiking Difficulty:

Hiking Rate:

☆ ☆ ☆ ☆ ☆

HIKING PARTNER(S)	CONTACT INFO

ADDITIONAL TRAIL NOTES

DATE:

LOCATION:

TRAIL INFORMATION

- Trail Name:
- Trail Type:
- Trail Distance:
- Altitude:
- Terrain Level:
- Entry/Parking Fees:
- Water Availability:
- Cell Phone Signal:

DETAILS

Weather/Temp:

Start Day/Time:

End Day/Time:

First Visit:

Return Visit:

Hiking Difficulty:

Hiking Rate:

☆ ☆ ☆ ☆ ☆

HIKING PARTNER(S)

CONTACT INFO

ADDITIONAL TRAIL NOTES

DATE:

LOCATION:

TRAIL INFORMATION

Trail Name:

Trail Type:

Trail Distance:

Altitude:

Terrain Level:

Entry/Parking Fees:

Water Availability:

Cell Phone Signal:

DETAILS

Weather/Temp:

Start Day/Time:

End Day/Time:

First Visit:

Return Visit:

Hiking Difficulty:

Hiking Rate:

☆ ☆ ☆ ☆ ☆

HIKING PARTNER(S)

CONTACT INFO

ADDITIONAL TRAIL NOTES

DATE:

LOCATION:

TRAIL INFORMATION

- Trail Name:
- Trail Type:
- Trail Distance:
- Altitude:
- Terrain Level:
- Entry/Parking Fees:
- Water Availability:
- Cell Phone Signal:

DETAILS

Weather/Temp:

Start Day/Time:

End Day/Time:

First Visit:

Return Visit:

Hiking Difficulty:

Hiking Rate:

☆ ☆ ☆ ☆ ☆

HIKING PARTNER(S)	CONTACT INFO

ADDITIONAL TRAIL NOTES

DATE:

LOCATION:

TRAIL INFORMATION

- Trail Name:
- Trail Type:
- Trail Distance:
- Altitude:
- Terrain Level:
- Entry/Parking Fees:
- Water Availability:
- Cell Phone Signal:

DETAILS

Weather/Temp:

Start Day/Time:

End Day/Time:

First Visit:

Return Visit:

Hiking Difficulty:

Hiking Rate:

☆ ☆ ☆ ☆ ☆

HIKING PARTNER(S)	CONTACT INFO

ADDITIONAL TRAIL NOTES

DATE:

LOCATION:

TRAIL INFORMATION

Trail Name:

Trail Type:

Trail Distance:

Altitude:

Terrain Level:

Entry/Parking Fees:

Water Availability:

Cell Phone Signal:

DETAILS

Weather/Temp:

Start Day/Time:

End Day/Time:

First Visit:

Return Visit:

Hiking Difficulty:

Hiking Rate:

☆ ☆ ☆ ☆ ☆

HIKING PARTNER(S)

CONTACT INFO

ADDITIONAL TRAIL NOTES

DATE:

LOCATION:

TRAIL INFORMATION

- Trail Name:
- Trail Type:
- Trail Distance:
- Altitude:
- Terrain Level:
- Entry/Parking Fees:
- Water Availability:
- Cell Phone Signal:

DETAILS

Weather/Temp:

Start Day/Time:

End Day/Time:

First Visit:

Return Visit:

Hiking Difficulty:

Hiking Rate:

☆ ☆ ☆ ☆ ☆

HIKING PARTNER(S)	CONTACT INFO

ADDITIONAL TRAIL NOTES

DATE:

LOCATION:

TRAIL INFORMATION

- Trail Name:
- Trail Type:
- Trail Distance:
- Altitude:
- Terrain Level:
- Entry/Parking Fees:
- Water Availability:
- Cell Phone Signal:

DETAILS

Weather/Temp:

Start Day/Time:

End Day/Time:

First Visit:

Return Visit:

Hiking Difficulty:

Hiking Rate:

☆   ☆   ☆   ☆   ☆

HIKING PARTNER(S)

CONTACT INFO

ADDITIONAL TRAIL NOTES

DATE:

LOCATION:

TRAIL INFORMATION

- Trail Name:
- Trail Type:
- Trail Distance:
- Altitude:
- Terrain Level:
- Entry/Parking Fees:
- Water Availability:
- Cell Phone Signal:

DETAILS

Weather/Temp:

Start Day/Time:

End Day/Time:

First Visit:

Return Visit:

Hiking Difficulty:

Hiking Rate:

☆   ☆   ☆   ☆   ☆

HIKING PARTNER(S)

CONTACT INFO

ADDITIONAL TRAIL NOTES

DATE:

LOCATION:

TRAIL INFORMATION

Trail Name:

Trail Type:

Trail Distance:

Altitude:

Terrain Level:

Entry/Parking Fees:

Water Availability:

Cell Phone Signal:

DETAILS

Weather/Temp:

Start Day/Time:

End Day/Time:

First Visit:

Return Visit:

Hiking Difficulty:

Hiking Rate:

☆ ☆ ☆ ☆ ☆

HIKING PARTNER(S)

CONTACT INFO

ADDITIONAL TRAIL NOTES

DATE:

LOCATION:

TRAIL INFORMATION

- Trail Name:
- Trail Type:
- Trail Distance:
- Altitude:
- Terrain Level:
- Entry/Parking Fees:
- Water Availability:
- Cell Phone Signal:

DETAILS

Weather/Temp:

Start Day/Time:

End Day/Time:

First Visit:

Return Visit:

Hiking Difficulty:

Hiking Rate:

☆ ☆ ☆ ☆ ☆

HIKING PARTNER(S)

CONTACT INFO

ADDITIONAL TRAIL NOTES

www.ingramcontent.com/pod-product-compliance
Lightning Source LLC
Chambersburg PA
CBHW040829300326
41914CB00059B/1301